From
Janice   2/2002

FAITH · HOPE AND LIGHT

FAITH · HOPE AND LIGHT
THE ART OF THE STAINED GLASS WINDOW

COURAGE
BOOKS

AN IMPRINT OF RUNNING PRESS
PHILADELPHIA · LONDON

Copyright © 1999 by Running Press
Printed in China
All rights reserved under the Pan-American and
International Copyright Conventions

*This book may not be reproduced in whole or in part in any form or by any means,
electronic or mechanical, including photocopying, recording, or by any information
storage and retrieval system now known or hereafter invented,
without written permission from the publisher.*

9   8   7   6   5   4   3   2   1
Digit on the right indicates the number of this printing.

Library of Congress Cataloging-in-publication Number 98-68514
ISBN 0-7624-0593-7

Cover design by Corinda Cook
Interior design by Mary Ann Liquori
Introduction by Sonya Beard
Edited by Yvette M. Chin
Pictures researched by Susan Oyama

This book may be ordered from the publisher. *But try your bookstore first!*

Published by Courage Books, an imprint of
Running Press Book Publishers
125 South Twenty-second Street
Philadelphia, Pennsylvania 19103–4399

Visit us on the web!
www.runningpress.com

CONTENTS

❖

❖

There are in the end three things that last: Faith, Hope, and Love, and the greatest of these is Love.

St. Paul (died c. 62–68 A.D.)
I Corinthians 13:13

Introduction

❖   ❖   ❖

Faith. Hope. Love. They are three simple words, yet they sum up the things that lend life meaning. This treasury of quotations and stained glass artwork contains reflections from a variety of thinkers—scientists, saints, artists, and poets. They speak from diverse eras and points of view, but their words all echo eternal themes—our relationships with other people and with our Creator and the ways in which we see, think, and act as we move through life. Like poignant words, stained glass can inspire your own reflections, or offer strength through the day.

Perhaps our earliest introduction to stained glass windows was during a grade school art assignment. Armed with a pair of scissors and our vivid imagination, our hope was that our mothers would hang our would-be masterpieces in the kitchen window. Our teacher began our journey into a meadow of creative tapestries by distributing sheets of black construction paper. Next, she instructed the class to carve out geometric designs, encouraging us to be daring and different. Then, we selected an array of vibrant and pastel sheets of tissue paper to fill in behind the geometric shapes. The teacher promised us the sun's golden rays would come shining through the sheer colors, and our art would dance with sparkling perfection at the mere hint of light. She challenged us to put nature's rainbows to shame.

And when the assignment was over, we had our own personal stained glass masterpiece worthy for any window in the house. It may not have been flawless, but the sun covered any imperfections we might have made. And with the sun glowing on your side, it was difficult to find anything more stunning.

Historically, stained glass dates back nearly 1,000 years, to the eleventh century. The early designs started out simple but became increasingly more detailed. One of the earliest works includes a piece titled *Head of Christ,* dating from the eleventh century, which portrays a simple Christ figure piously watching over his followers. The windows at the Canterbury Cathedral, a pilgrimage site since 1173, depict the lives of saints, with powerful hues emphasizing dramatic messages.

It is important to point out that stained glass was not exclusively displayed in synagogues and cathedrals. One of the most important contemporary connoisseurs of stained glass art fashioned his designs as lamp shades. Instead of solar illumination, a light bulb worked just as well and made a fortune for Louis Comfort Tiffany in the late 1800s. In his signature stained glass patterns, Tiffany also made vases, cigarette boxes, and tiles for walls and floors. Some more modern-day masterpieces were post–World War II works, including pieces by the famed artist Marc Chagall, whose creations are on display worldwide. Now enthusiasts can see stained glass artwork celebrating everything from Elvis to multicultural pride. Yesterday and today, the objectives for stained glass have remained constant. They are best at telling picture-book stories, sometimes tragic, sometimes joyous.

Without any light to support it, stained glass is but a dull painting, like a solemn novel without a climax. When it joins forces with that flame in the sky, it becomes a triumphant oration. Whether the works are modern or classical, they capture the attention and the hearts of anyone who basks in their glorious presence. Their beauty is undeniable. Something magical takes place—a feeling, not an experience, that sends a chill through your veins that is soon followed by a sense of warmth.

It's the feeling our mother experienced when we presented her with our very own stained glass masterpiece.

NEXT PAGE: *AN EMPEROR OF THE HOLY ROMAN EMPIRE;* MUSÉE DE L'OEUVRE DE NOTRE DAME, STRASBOURG, FRANCE; 12TH CENTURY

FAITH

God is a writer and we are both the heroes and the readers.

Isaac Bashevis Singer (1904–1992)
Polish-born American writer

God had made many doors opening into truth which

He opens to all who knock upon them with hands of faith.

❖   ❖   ❖

Kahlil Gibran (1883–1931)
Lebanese writer and artist

Opposite: *Gerlachus, Painter of the Moses and Aaron Window*, a self-portrait by Gerlachus; from the Praemonstratensian Monastery, now in the Westfaelisches Landesmuseum, Muenster, Germany; 12th century

I never saw a moor,

I never saw the sea;

Yet know I how the heather looks,

And what a wave must be.

I never spoke with God,

Nor visited in heaven;

Yet certain am I of the spot

As if the chart were given.

EMILY DICKINSON (1830–1886)
AMERICAN POET

OPPOSITE: *NOAH EMBARKING UPON THE ARK*, CHURCH OF SAINT ANIETUS AND SAINT NEOT, CORNWALL, UNITED KINGDOM, 15TH CENTURY

EVERYTHING HAPPENING, GREAT AND SMALL, IS A PARABLE WHEREBY

GOD SPEAKS TO US, AND THE ART OF LIFE IS TO GET THE MESSAGE.

❖ ❖ ❖

Malcolm Muggeridge (1903–1990)
English journalist and writer

I would rather live in a world where my life is surrounded by mystery

than live in a world so small that my mind could comprehend it.

HARRY E. FOSDICK (1878–1969)
AMERICAN CLERGYMAN AND PROFESSOR

OPPOSITE: *KING SOLOMON HOLDING THE TEMPLE* BY SIR EDWARD BURNE-JONES; LEIGH, STAFFORDSHIRE, UNITED KINGDOM; 19TH CENTURY

IS not prayer a study of truth, a sally of the soul into the unfound

infinite? No man ever prayed heartily without learning something.

❖ ❖ ❖

RALPH WALDO EMERSON (1803–1882)
AMERICAN ESSAYIST AND POET

OPPOSITE: *ANNUNCIATION* BY SIR EDWARD BURNE-JONES AND MICHAEL HALLIDAY;
SAINT COLUMBA'S CHURCH, TOPCLIFFE, NORTH YORKSHIRE, UNITED KINGDOM; 19TH CENTURY

To believe in God for me is to feel that there is a God,

not a dead one, or a stuffed one, but a living one,

who with irresistible force urges us towards more loving.

❖   ❖   ❖

Vincent van Gogh (1853–1890)
Dutch painter

The belief that becomes truth for me . . . is that which allows me the best use of my strength, the best means of putting my virtues into action.

André Gide (1869–1951)
French writer and critic

Opposite: *Saint George;* German origin, now in the Hermitage, St. Petersburg, Russia; 15th century

HAVING FAITH IN GOD

DID NOT MEAN SITTING BACK AND DOING NOTHING. IT MEANT BELIEVING THAT

YOU WOULD FIND SUCCESS IF YOU DID YOUR BEST HONESTLY AND ENERGETICALLY.

❖ ◇ ❖

Ken Follett
English writer

Opposite: *Head of Christ*; from the Abbey Church of Saint Peter and Saint Paul, Wissembourg, now in the Musée de l'Oeuvre de Notre Dame, Strasbourg, France; 11th century

It fortifies my soul to know

That, though I perish,

Truth is so:

That Howsoe'er I stray and range,

Whate'er I do, Thou dost not change.

I steadier step when I recall

That, if I slip, Thou dost not fall.

ARTHUR HUGH CLOUGH (1819–1861)
ENGLISH POET

KNOWLEDGE IS PROUD THAT HE HAS LEARNED SO MUCH;

WISDOM IS HUMBLE THAT HE KNOWS NO MORE.

✧   ✧   ✧

William Cowper (1731–1800)
English poet

OPPOSITE: *FIGURES OF CHRIST* BY JOHN PIPER; OUNDLE SCHOOL CHAPEL, NORTHAMPTONSHIRE, UNITED KINGDOM; 20TH CENTURY

Nothing before,

nothing behind;

the steps of faith

fall on the seeming

void and find

the rock beneath.

JOHN GREENLEAF WHITTIER (1807–1892)
AMERICAN POET

FAITH AND DOUBT

BOTH ARE NEEDED—NOT AS ANTAGONISTS,

BUT WORKING SIDE BY SIDE—TO TAKE US AROUND THE UNKNOWN CURVE.

❖ ❖ ❖

Lillian Smith (1897–1966)
American novelist and educator

OPPOSITE: *ADAM IN THE GARDEN OF EDEN;* MUSÉE DE L'OEUVRE DE NOTRE DAME, STRASBOURG, FRANCE; 15TH CENTURY

Living faith is a rock with roots.

Puzant Kevork Thomajan
20th-century American writer and poet

Even the merest gesture is holy if it is filled with faith.

❖   ❖   ❖

Franz Kafka (1883–1924)
Austrian writer

Opposite: *Love Draws Strength*; Thermal Baths, Aix-les-Bains, France; 19th century

To us also,

through every star,

through every blade

of grass, is not God

made visible if

we will open our

minds and eyes?

❖   ❖   ❖

Thomas Carlyle (1795–1881)
Scottish essayist and historian

It is only with the heart that one can see rightly;

what is essential is invisible to the eye.

Antoine de Saint-Exupéry (1900–1944)
French Aviator and Writer

Opposite: *Meeting of the Visible and the Invisible* by Jean Cocteau; Milly-la-Fôret, France; 20th century

PEOPLE SEE GOD EVERY DAY,

THEY JUST DON'T RECOGNIZE HIM.

Pearl Bailey (1918–1990)
American singer

Golden hours of vision come to us in this present life when we are at our best.

✧　✧　✧

Charles Fletcher Dole (1845–1927)
American clergyman and author

Opposite: *Dorigen* by Sir Edward Burne-Jones; Birmingham City Museum and Art Gallery, Birmingham, United Kingdom; 19th century

33

Faith is to believe, on the word of God, what we do not see, and its reward is to

SEE AND ENJOY WHAT WE BELIEVE.

St. Augustine of Hippo (354–430)
Early Christian theologian

. . . I do not seek to understand that I may believe, but I believe in order to understand.

❖ ❖ ❖

St. Anselm of Canterbury (1034–1109)
Italian-born English theologian

Opposite: *Sarah d'Avigdor-Goldsmid Memorial Window* by Marc Chagall; All Saints Church, Tudeley, Kent, United Kingdom; 20th century

34

Glorious indeed is the world of God around us, but more

glorious the world of God within us. There lies the land of song: there lies the poet's native land.

HENRY WADSWORTH LONGFELLOW (1807–1882)
AMERICAN POET

TO GET INTO THE CORE OF GOD AT HIS GREATEST, ONE MUST

FIRST GET INTO THE CORE OF HIMSELF AT HIS LEAST, FOR NO

ONE CAN KNOW GOD WHO HAS NOT FIRST KNOWN HIMSELF.

❖   ❖   ❖

Johannes Eckhard (c. 1260–1327)
German vicar and mystic

OPPOSITE: WINDOW BY JOHN PIPER, BASED ON *TYMPANUM* AT NEUILLY-EN-DONJON,
ALLIER, FRANCE; ROBINSON COLLEGE, CAMBRIDGE, CAMBRIDGESHIRE, UNITED KINGDOM; 20TH CENTURY

. . . I, who am curious about each,

am not curious about God—

I hear and behold God in every object,

yet understand God not in the least.

Walt Whitman (1819–1892)
American poet

Opposite: *Angels, Saints, and Apostles in a Choir Window*; Cologne Cathedral, Germany; 13th century

...A person who is religiously enlightened appears

to be to me one who has . . . liberated himself from the fetters of his selfish desires and is preoccupied with thoughts,

feelings, and aspirations to which he clings because of their superpersonal value.

ALBERT EINSTEIN (1879–1955)
GERMAN-BORN AMERICAN PHYSICIST

GOD HAD DELEGATED HIMSELF TO A MILLION DEPUTIES.

❖   ❖   ❖

Ralph Waldo Emerson (1803–1882)
American essayist and poet

OPPOSITE: *THE SONS AND DAUGHTERS OF THE DONORS*; CHURCH OF SAINT MATTHEW, MORLEY, DERBYSHIRE, UNITED KINGDOM; 15TH CENTURY

Any God I ever felt in church I brought in with me.

And I think all the other folks did too.

They come to church to share God, not find God.

Alice Walker
American writer

Miracles are not contrary to nature, but only contrary to what we know about nature.

❖ ❖ ❖

St. Augustine of Hippo (354–430)
Early Christian theologian

OPPOSITE: *The Creation of the Birds and the Animals*; Saint Florentin, near Auxerre, France; 15th century

sancta margarita

Half of the confusion

in the world

comes from not knowing

how little we need . . .

I live more simply now,

and with more peace.

RICHARD EVELYN BYRD (1888–1957)
AMERICAN NAVAL OFFICER AND EXPLORER

IT IS DIFFICULT TO BELIEVE IN GOD,

NOT BECAUSE HE IS SO FAR OFF,

BUT BECAUSE HE IS SO NEAR.

William Hale White (1831–1913)
English novelist

OPPOSITE: *SAINT MARGARET* BY J. H. DEARLE; SAINT PETER'S CHURCH, BRAMLEY, YORKSHIRE, UNITED KINGDOM; 19TH CENTURY
NEXT PAGE: *MASTER OF SAINT SEVRIN SHOWING THE TEMPTATION OF CHRIST*; IN THE STYLE OF THE COLOGNE
SCHOOL, GERMANY, NOW IN THE VICTORIA AND ALBERT MUSEUM, LONDON, UNITED KINGDOM; 16TH CENTURY

HOPE

God brings no man into the conflicts of life to desert him. Every man has a friend in heaven

whose resources are unlimited; and on Him he may call at any hour and find sympathy and assistance.

❖ ❖ ❖

ROBERT HUGH MORRIS (1734–1806)
AMERICAN FINANCIER AND POLITICIAN   ·

OPPOSITE: *SCENE FROM THE LIFE OF THOMAS À BECKET;* FROM THE CANTERBURY CATHEDRAL, NOW IN A PRIVATE COLLECTION, UNITED KINGDOM; 13TH CENTURY

SCVLPTVRE

et nothing disturb thee;

Let nothing dismay thee;

All things pass;

God never changes.

Patience attains

All that it strives for.

He who has God

Finds he lacks nothing;

God alone suffices.

St. Teresa de Cepeda (1515–1582)
Spanish religious leader

Opposite: *Sculpture*, designed by Gaetano Meo, made by James Powell and Sons; Bonhams, London, United Kingdom; 19th century

...WHEN LIFE KNOCKS YOU TO YOUR KNEES—

WELL, THAT'S THE BEST POSITION IN WHICH TO PRAY, ISN'T IT?

Ethel Barrymore (1879–1959)
American actress

Heaven is full of answers to prayers for which no one ever bothered to ask.

❖   ❖   ❖

BILLY GRAHAM
AMERICAN EVANGELIST

OPPOSITE: *GIDEON AND THE SIGN OF THE FLEECE*; GERMAN CHURCH; C. 16TH–18TH CENTURY

I never knew a night so black

Light failed to follow on its track.

I never knew a storm so gray

It failed to have its clearing day.

I never knew such black despair

That there was not a rift somewhere.

I never knew an hour so drear

Love could not fill it full of cheer!

John Kendrick Bangs (1862–1922)
American writer and humorist

Opposite: *Saint Peter's Lack of Faith*; Tewkesbury Abbey, Gloucestershire, United Kingdom; 19th century

THERE'S A DIVINITY THAT SHAPES OUR ENDS,

ROUGH-HEW THEM HOW WE WILL.

William Shakespeare (1564–1616)
English dramatist and poet

I know not where his islands lift

Their fronded palms in air;

I only know I cannot drift

Beyond His love and care.

✦   ✦   ✦

JOHN GREENLEAF WHITTIER (1807–1892)
AMERICAN WRITER

OPPOSITE: DETAIL FROM *THE NATIVITY* BY LIPPI DA LORENZO DA PELAGO; PRATO CATHEDRAL, PRATO, ITALY; 15TH CENTURY

Hope humbly then; with trembling pinions soar . . .

What future bliss, he gives not thee to know,

But gives that Hope to be thy blessing now.

Hope springs eternal in the human breast:

Man never Is, but always To be blest.

The soul, uneasy, and confin'd from home,

Rests and espatiates in a life to come.

❖   ❖   ❖

ALEXANDER POPE (1688–1744)
ENGLISH POET

OPPOSITE: DETAIL FROM *THE ARK OF THE COVENANT*; CHURCH OF SAINT DENIS, PARIS, FRANCE; 12TH CENTURY

The word hope I take for faith; and indeed

hope is nothing else but the constancy of faith.

JOHN CALVIN (1509–1564)
FRENCH THEOLOGIAN AND REFORMER

GOD LIES AHEAD. I CONVINCE MYSELF AND CONSTANTLY REPEAT TO MYSELF

THAT HE DEPENDS ON US. IT IS THROUGH US THAT GOD IS ACHIEVED.

❖ ❖ ❖

André Gide (1869–1951)
French writer and critic

OPPOSITE: *CHRIST WITH LITTLE CHILDREN* BY LOUIS COMFORT TIFFANY; CHURCH OF SAINT ANDREW, KIMBOLTON, CAMBRIDGESHIRE, UNITED KINGDOM; 20TH CENTURY

60

It is one of my favorite thoughts, that God

manifests himself to mankind in all wise, good,

humble, generous, great, and magnanimous men.

Johann Kaspar Lavater (1741–1801)
Swiss writer, philosopher, and theologian

The wonderful thing about saints is that they were human.

They lost their tempers, scolded God, were egotistical or testy

or impatient in their turns, made mistakes and regretted them.

Still they went on doggedly blundering toward heaven.

❖ ❖ ❖

Phyllis McGinley (1905–1977)
American writer

Opposite: *Christ and the Four Evangelists* by Henry Holiday; Buckland Monachoram Church, Devon, United Kingdom; 19th century

When two people loved each other

they worked together always, two against the world, a little company. Joy was shared;

trouble was split. You had an ally, somewhere, who was helping.

PAUL GALLICO (1897–1976)
AMERICAN JOURNALIST AND WRITER

SAID A WISE MAN TO ONE IN DEEP SORROW, "I DID NOT COME

TO COMFORT YOU; GOD ONLY CAN DO THAT, BUT I DID COME

TO SAY HOW DEEPLY AND TENDERLY I FEEL FOR YOU. . . ."

❖ ❖ ❖

Tryon Edwards (1809–1894)
American clergyman and writer

OPPOSITE: *THE LOVE POTION*, FROM THE STORY OF TRISTAN AND ISOLDE, DESIGNED BY DANTE GABRIEL ROSSETTI, MADE BY WILLIAM MORRIS
AND CO., ORIGINALLY FROM THE HARDEN GRANGE, NOW IN THE BRADFORD ART GALLERIES AND MUSEUMS, YORKSHIRE, UNITED KINGDOM; 19TH CENTURY

When you get to your wit's end, you'll find God lives there.

ANONYMOUS

IF SOMEONE LISTENS,

OR STRETCHES OUT A HAND, OR WHISPERS A KIND WORD OF

ENCOURAGEMENT, OR ATTEMPTS TO UNDERSTAND A LONELY

PERSON, EXTRAORDINARY THINGS BEGIN TO HAPPEN.

✧ ✧ ✧

Loretta Girzartis
American writer and educator

OPPOSITE: DETAIL FROM *THE ANNUNCIATION*; ELY STAINED GLASS MUSEUM, ELY CATHEDRAL, CAMBRIDGESHIRE, UNITED KINGDOM; 14TH CENTURY

Reflect upon your present blessings, of which every

man has many; not on your past misfortune, of which all men have some.

CHARLES DICKENS (1812–1870)
ENGLISH NOVELIST

IN SPITE OF EVERYTHING

I STILL BELIEVE PEOPLE ARE REALLY GOOD AT HEART.

❖   ❖   ❖

Anne Frank (1929–1945)
German Jewish diarist

OPPOSITE: PSALM 150, OH PRAISE GOD IN HIS HOLINESS BY MARC CHAGALL; CHICHESTER CATHEDRAL, SUSSEX, UNITED KINGDOM; 20TH CENTURY

Now is no time to think of what you do not have.

Think of what you can do with what there is.

Ernest Hemingway (1899–1961)
American writer

We should find God in what we do know, not in what we don't;

not in outstanding problems, but in those we have already solved.

✧ ✧ ✧

Dietrich Bonhoeffer (1906–1945)
German theologian

OPPOSITE: *December*, from the *Labors of the Months* series; Victoria and Albert Museum, London, United Kingdom; 15th century

Life comes with a warranty.

❖   ❖   ❖

Allan Gurganus
American writer

Never bear more than one kind of trouble at a time.

Some people bear three—all they have had,

all they have now, and all they expect to have.

Edward Everett Hale (1822–1909)
American writer and clergyman

Opposite: Detail from *Temptation in the Desert*, from the Troyes Cathedral, Paris,
France, now in the Victoria and Albert Museum, London, United Kingdom; 13th century

72

THE MOST SOLID COMFORT ONE CAN FALL BACK UPON IS THE THOUGHT THAT THE

BUSINESS OF ONE'S LIFE IS TO HELP IN SOME SMALL WAY TO REDUCE THE SUM OF

IGNORANCE, DEGRADATION, AND MISERY ON THE FACE OF THIS BEAUTIFUL EARTH.

❖ ❖ ❖

George Eliot (1819–1880)
English writer

OPPOSITE: DETAIL FROM *NOAH IN HIS ARK;* FROM THE CHURCH OF WIMPFFEN IM TALE, NOW IN THE HESSISCHES LANDESMUSEUM, DARMSTADT, GERMANY; 13TH CENTURY

75

NEVER THINK THAT GOD'S DELAYS ARE GOD'S DENIALS.

HOLD ON; HOLD FAST; HOLD OUT. PATIENCE IS GENIUS.

Comte Georges Louis Leclerc de Buffon (1707–1788)
French naturalist and writer

It takes no more time to see the good side of life than it takes to see the bad.

❖ ❖ ❖

JIMMY BUFFETT
AMERICAN SINGER AND WRITER

OPPOSITE: DETAIL FROM *THE LEGEND OF SAINT NICHOLAS AND THE TEMPTATION OF CHRIST;* CATHEDRAL OF SAINT PETER AND SAINT PAUL, TROYES, FRANCE; 13TH CENTURY

Patient waiting is often the highest way of doing God's will.

JEREMY COLLIER (1650–1726)
ENGLISH BISHOP AND HISTORIAN

I HAVE LIVED TO THANK GOD THAT ALL MY PRAYERS HAVE NOT BEEN ANSWERED.

❖   ❖   ❖

Jean Ingelow (1820–1897)
English poet

OPPOSITE: DETAIL FROM *MARGARETE, GOVERNESS OF THE NETHERLANDS*; ÉGLISE DE BROU, BOURG-EN-BRESSE, FRANCE; 16TH CENTURY

A single grateful thought raised to heaven is the most perfect prayer.

❖ ❖ ❖

Gotthold Ephraim Lessing (1729–1781)
German dramatist and critic

In prayer it is better to have

heart without words, than words without heart.

John Bunyan (1628–1688)
English preacher and writer

Opposite: *Two Kneeling Angels; Potosi, Bolivia; 19th century*

WHATSOEVER WE BEG OF GOD, LET US ALSO

WORK FOR IT.

Jeremy Taylor (1613–1667)
English prelate and author

To look up and not down,

To look forward and not back,

To look out and not in, and

To lend a hand.

EDWARD EVERETT HALE (1822–1909)
AMERICAN CLERGYMAN AND WRITER

OPPOSITE: *RUTH GLEANING* BY R. T. BAYNE; SCULTHORPE CHURCH, NORFOLK, UNITED KINGDOM; 19TH CENTURY

JOY IS OF THE

WILL WHICH LABOURS,

WHICH OVERCOMES OBSTACLES,

WHICH KNOWS TRIUMPH.

❖   ❖   ❖

William Butler Yeats (1865–1939)
Irish poet and playwright

Joy is the serious business of heaven.

❖   ❖   ❖

C. S. Lewis (1898–1963)
English scholar and writer

Laughter is one of the best things

that God has given us,

AND WITH HEARTY LAUGHTER

Neither malice nor indecency can exist.

Stanley Baldwin (1867–1947)
English politician and writer

HAPPINESS SNEAKS IN

THROUGH A DOOR

YOU DIDN'T KNOW

YOU LEFT OPEN.

❖ ❖ ❖

John Barrymore (1882–1942)
American actor

Laugh and grow strong.

St. Ignatius of Loyola (1491–1556)
Spanish religious leader

Opposite: *Saint Cecilia with Palm and Bell*; Church of All Saints, Langport, Somerset, United Kingdom; 15th century
Next page: *Honeymoon of King René of Anjou* by Sir Edward Burne-Jones and
Dante Gabriel Rossetti; Victoria and Albert Museum, London, United Kingdom; 19th century

89

✦ ✦ LOVE ✦

✦

We can do no great things—only small things with great love.

MOTHER TERESA (1910–1997)
FOUNDER, MISSIONARIES OF CHARITY

JOY IS LOVE EXALTED, PEACE IS LOVE IN REPOSE; LONG-SUFFERING IS LOVE ENDURING;

GENTLENESS IS LOVE IN SOCIETY; GOODNESS IS LOVE IN ACTION; FAITH IS LOVE ON THE

BATTLEFIELD; MEEKNESS IS LOVE IN SCHOOL; AND TEMPERANCE IS LOVE IN TRAINING.

❖   ❖   ❖

Dwight L. Moody (1837–1899)
American evangelist and educator

OPPOSITE: DETAIL FROM *CHRIST IN MAJESTY*, THE SOUTHERN ROSE WINDOW; CHARTRES CATHEDRAL, FRANCE; 13TH CENTURY

Love is indestructible,

Its holy flame forever burneth;

From heaven it came, to heaven returneth.

ROBERT SOUTHEY (1774–1843)
BRITISH POET

OPPOSITE: DETAIL FROM PRODIGAL SON, CURLEW RIVER, AND THE BURNING FIERY FURNACE BY JOHN PIPER; ALDEBURGH CHURCH, SUFFOLK, UNITED KINGDOM; 20TH CENTURY

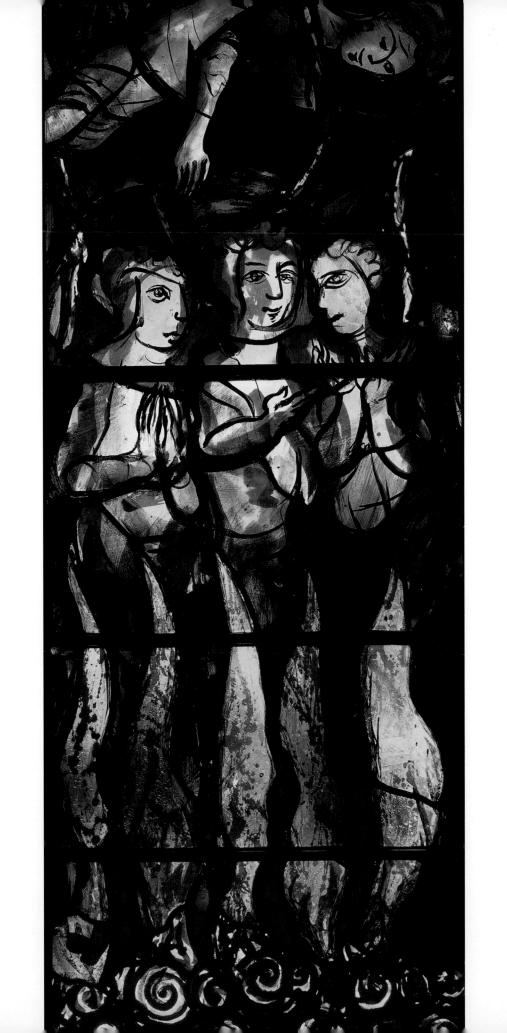

THE LORD'S GOODNESS SURROUNDS US AT EVERY

MOMENT. I WALK THROUGH IT ALMOST WITH

DIFFICULTY, AS THROUGH THICK GRASS AND FLOWERS.

R. W. Barbour
American writer

God, from a beautiful necessity, is love.

❖   ❖   ❖

MARTIN FARQUHAR TUPPER (1810–1889)
ENGLISH WRITER

He prayeth well who loveth well

Both man and bird and beast.

He prayeth best who loveth best

All things both great and small;

For the dear God who loveth us,

He made and loveth all.

SAMUEL TAYLOR COLERIDGE (1772–1834)
BRITISH POET AND CRITIC

FOR THE GREAT SPIRIT IS EVERYWHERE: HE HEARS

WHATEVER IS IN OUR MINDS AND HEARTS, AND IT IS

NOT NECESSARY TO SPEAK TO HIM IN A LOUD VOICE.

❖ ❖ ❖

Black Elk (1863–1950)
Oglala Sioux holy man

LOVE IS THE ONLY PRAYER.

Marion Zimmer Bradley
American writer

Only through love can we attain to communion with God.

❖   ❖   ❖

ALBERT SCHWEITZER (1875–1965)
FRENCH PHYSICIAN, PHILOSOPHER, AND MUSICIAN

OPPOSITE: DETAIL FROM *THE VIRGIN AND CHILD*; CHURCH OF SAINT MARY AND ALL SAINTS, RIVENHALL, ESSEX, UNITED KINGDOM; 12TH CENTURY

[Infinite love] is a weapon of matchless potency. It is the *summum bonum* of life. It is an attribute of the brave, in fact it is their all. It does not come within the reach of the coward. It is no wooden or lifeless dogma but a living and life-giving force. It is the special attribute of the heart.

MOHANDAS GANDHI (1869–1948)
INDIAN POLITICAL LEADER

Love seeks one thing only: the good of the one loved.

It leaves all the other secondary effects to take care of

themselves. Love, therefore, is its own reward.

❖ ❖ ❖

THOMAS MERTON (1915–1968)
AMERICAN CLERGYMAN AND WRITER

LOVE IS A FAITH,

AND ONE FAITH LEADS TO ANOTHER.

Henri Frédéric Amiel (1821–1881)
Swiss poet and philosopher

OPPOSITE: *MADONNA AND CHILD*, SAMMLUNG DES REIDESFREIHERRN VON STEIN, KAPPENBURG, GERMANY; 14TH CENTURY

IT WERE WISER TO SPEAK LESS OF GOD,

WHOM WE CANNOT UNDERSTAND,

AND MORE OF EACH OTHER,

WHOM WE MAY UNDERSTAND.

YET I WOULD HAVE YOU KNOW

THAT WE ARE THE BREATH AND THE FRAGRANCE OF GOD.

WE ARE GOD, IN LEAF, IN FLOWER,

AND OFTENTIMES IN FRUIT.

Kahlil Gibran (1883–1931)
Lebanese writer and artist

THOSE WHO BRING SUNSHINE TO THE LIVES OF OTHERS CANNOT KEEP IT FROM THEMSELVES.

Sir James M. Barrie (1860–1937)
Scottish novelist and dramatist

When I think of God, my heart is so full of joy that the notes leap and dance as they

leave my pen; and since God has given me a cheerful heart, I serve him with a cheerful spirit.

FRANZ JOSEPH HAYDN (1732–1809)
AUSTRIAN COMPOSER

OPPOSITE: *JOURNEY OF THE PRODIGAL SON* BY DIDRON OF PARIS; CHURCH OF SAINT MARY, FELTWELL, NORFOLK, UNITED KINGDOM; 19TH CENTURY

IF A FRIEND IS IN TROUBLE,

DON'T ANNOY HIM BY ASKING IF THERE IS ANYTHING YOU CAN DO.

THINK UP SOMETHING APPROPRIATE AND DO IT.

❖   ❖   ❖

Edgar Watson Howe (1853–1937)
American journalist and author

OPPOSITE: DETAIL FROM *SAINT DAMIAN HEALING A LAME* BY THE MASTER OF SAINT FRANCIS; UPPER CHURCH, SAN FRANCESCO ASSISI, ASSISI, ITALY; 13TH CENTURY

111

The water does not flow until the faucet is turned on.

Louis L'Amour (1908–1988)
American author and screenwriter

May I tell you why it seems to me a good thing for us to

remember wrong that has been done us? That we may forgive it.

❖   ❖   ❖

Charles Dickens (1812–1870)
English novelist

Opposite: *Untitled* by Marc Chagall; All Saints Church, Tudeley, Kent, United Kingdom; 20th century

Love in its essence is spiritual fire.

EMMANUEL SWEDENBORG (1688–1772)
SWEDISH SCIENTIST AND PHILOSOPHER

OPPOSITE: *MOSES AND THE GOLDEN CALF*; VICTORIA AND ALBERT MUSEUM, LONDON, UNITED KINGDOM; 16TH CENTURY

LOVE DOESN'T JUST SIT THERE, LIKE A STONE, IT HAS TO

BE MADE, LIKE BREAD; RE-MADE ALL THE TIME, MADE NEW.

❖ ❖ ❖

Ursula K. LeGuin
American writer

The simplest and shortest ethical precept is to be served by

others as little as possible, and to serve others as much as possible.

LEO TOLSTOY (1828–1910)
RUSSIAN WRITER AND PHILOSOPHER

OPPOSITE: *SOWER* WINDOW; CANTERBURY CATHEDRAL, KENT, UNITED KINGDOM; C. 12TH–13TH CENTURY

GOD IS A VERB, NOT A NOUN.

R. Buckminster Fuller (1895–1983)
American engineer

We must not only give what we have; we must also give what we are.

❖   ❖   ❖

Désiré Joseph Mercier (1851–1926)
Belgian prelate and philosopher

Opposite: *The Prophet Daniel*; Victoria and Albert Museum, London, United Kingdom; 15th century

Guard well within yourself that treasure, kindness.

Know how to give without hesitation,

how to lose without regret,

how to acquire without meanness.

❖ ❖ ❖

George Sand (1804–1876)
French writer

I have found the paradox that if I love until it hurts, then

there is no hurt, but only more love.

MOTHER TERESA (1910–1997)
FOUNDER, MISSIONARIES OF CHARITY

OPPOSITE: *THE NATIVITY* BY SIR EDWARD BURNE-JONES; HUISH EPISCOPI, SOMERSET, UNITED KINGDOM; 19TH CENTURY

If I can put one touch

OF A ROSY SUNSET

INTO THE LIFE OF ANY MAN OR WOMAN,

I shall feel that I have

WORKED WITH GOD.

Henry David Thoreau (1817–1862)
American writer and naturalist

That which we love, we come to resemble.

✧   ✧   ✧

St. Bernard of Clairvaux (1091–1153)
French religious leader

Opposite: *Creation of the Sun and Moon;* Saint Florentin, near Auxerre, France; 15th century

All that we send into the lives of others comes back into our own.

❖   ❖   ❖

Edwin Markham (1852–1940)
American poet and educator

Opposite: *The Nativity*, designed by Domenico Ghirlandaio; Santa Maria delle Carceri, Prato, Italy; 15th century

Front cover: *Journey of the Prodigal Son* (1859), by Didron of Paris. Church of Saint Mary, Feltwell, Norfolk, United Kingdom; Bridgeman Art Library, London and New York.

Back cover: *Angels, Saints, and Apostles in a Choir Window* (13th century). Cologne Cathedral, Germany; Erich Lessing/Art Resource, New York.

FAITH

p. 8: *An Emperor of the Holy Roman Empire* (late-12th century). Musée de l'Oeuvre de Notre Dame, Strasbourg, France; Erich Lessing/Art Resource, New York.

p. 11: *Gerlachus, Painter of the Moses and Aaron Window*, detail (c. 1150), self-portrait by Gerlachus. Originally from the Praemonstratensian Monastery. Westfaelisches Landesmuseum, Muenster, Germany; Erich Lessing/Art Resource, New York.

p. 12: *Noah Embarking Upon the Ark*, detail (15th century). Church of Saint Anietus and Saint Neot, Cornwall, United Kingdom; Bridgeman Art Library, London and New York.

p. 15: *King Solomon Holding the Temple* (1890), by Sir Edward Burne-Jones (1833–98). Leigh, Staffordshire, United Kingdom; Ann S. Dean, Brighton/Bridgeman Art Library, London and New York.

p. 16: *Annunciation* (19th century), designed by Sir Edward Burne-Jones (1833–98) and Michael Halliday. Saint Columba's Church, Topcliffe, North Yorkshire, United Kingdom; Bridgeman Art Library, London and New York.

p. 19: *Saint George* (1400–10), Southern German. Hermitage, St. Petersburg, Russia; Bridgeman Art Library, London and New York.

p. 20: *Head of Christ* (c. 1070). Originally from the Abbey Church of Saint Peter and Saint Paul, Wissembourg. Musée de l'Oeuvre de Notre Dame, Strasbourg, France; Bridgeman Art Library, London and New York.

p. 23: *Figures of Christ* (1954), by John Piper. Oundle School Chapel, Northamptonshire, United Kingdom; Bridgeman Art Library, London and New York.

p. 24: *Adam in the Garden of Eden* (15th century). Musée de l'Oeuvre de Notre Dame, Strasbourg, France; Peter Willi/Bridgeman Art Library, London and New York.

p. 27: *Love Draws Strength* (1890s). Thermal Baths, Aix-les-Bains, France; Erich Lessing/Art Resource, New York.

p. 28: *Meeting of the Visible and the Invisible* (1958), by Jean Cocteau (1889–1963). Milly-la-Fôret, France; Bridgeman Art Library, London and New York. © 2000 Artists Rights Society (ARS), New York/ADAGP, Paris.

p. 31: *Untitled* (20th century), by Georges Braque (1882–1963). Fondation Maeght, Saint Paul de Vence, France; Bridgeman Art Library, London and New York. © 2000 Artists Rights Society (ARS), New York/ADAGP, Paris.

p. 32: *Dorigen* (c. 1876), designed by Sir Edward Burne-Jones (1833–98). Birmingham City Museum and Art Gallery, Birmingham, United Kingdom; Bridgeman Art Library, London and New York.

p. 35: *Sarah d'Avigdor-Goldsmid Memorial Window*, detail (1963), by Marc Chagall (1887–1985). All Saints Church, Tudeley, Kent, United Kingdom; Bridgeman Art Library, London and New York. © 2000 Artists Rights Society (ARS), New York/ADAGP, Paris.

p. 36: *Window based on Tympanum* at Neuilly-en-Donjon, Allier, France (1980), by John Piper (1903–92). Robinson College, Cambridge, Cambridgeshire, United Kingdom; Bridgeman Art Library, London and New York.

p. 39: *Angels, Saints, and Apostles in a Choir Window* (13th century). Cologne Cathedral, Germany; Erich Lessing/Art Resource, New York.

p. 40: *The Sons and Daughters of the Donors* (15th century). Church of Saint Matthew, Morley, Derbyshire, United Kingdom; Bridgeman Art Library, London and New York.

p. 43: *The Creation of the Birds and the Animals* (15th century). Saint Florentin, near Auxerre, France; Bridgeman Art Library, London and New York.

p. 44: *Saint Margaret* (1882), by J. H. Dearle. Saint Peter's Church, Bramley, Yorkshire, United Kingdom; The Fine Art Society, London/Bridgeman Art Library, London and New York.

HOPE

p. 46: *Master of Saint Sevrin showing the Temptation of Christ* (first-half of 16th century) in the style of the Cologne School, Germany. Victoria and Albert Museum, London, United Kingdom; Bridgeman Art Library, London and New York.

p. 48: *Scene from the Life of Saint Thomas à Becket* (c. 1220). Originally from the Canterbury Cathedral, Kent, United Kingdom. Private collection; Bridgeman Art Library, London and New York.

p. 50: *Sculpture* (c. 1890), design attributed to Gaetano Meo, made by James Powell and Sons. Bonhams, London, United Kingdom; Bridgeman Art Library, London and New York.

p. 53: *Gideon and the Sign of the Fleece* (c. 16th–18th century), German. German Church; Bridgeman Art Library, London and New York.

p. 54: *Saint Peter's Lack of Faith* (19th century). Tewkesbury Abbey, Gloucestershire, United Kingdom; Ann S. Dean, Brighton/ Bridgeman Art Library, London and New York.

p. 57: *The Nativity*, detail (c. 1459), from a design by Lippi da Lorenzo da Pelago. Prato Cathedral, Italy; Bridgeman Art Library, London and New York.

p. 58: *The Ark of the Covenant*, detail (12th century). Church of Saint Denis, Paris, France; Peter Willi/Bridgeman Art Library, London and New York.

p. 61: *Christ with Little Children*, detail (1902), by Louis Comfort Tiffany. Church of Saint Andrew, Kimbolton, Cambridgeshire, United Kingdom; Bridgeman Art Library, London and New York.

p. 62: *Christ and the Four Evangelists* (1870), by Henry Holiday (1839–1927). Buckland Monachoram Church, Devon, United Kingdom; Bridgeman Art Library, London and New York.

p. 65: *The Love Potion*, from the Story of Tristan and Isolde (19th century), designed by Dante Gabriel Rossetti (1828–82), made by William Morris & Co. Originally from Harden Grange, near Bingley, Yorkshire. Bradford Art Galleries and Museums, West Yorkshire, United Kingdom; Bridgeman Art Library, London and New York.

p. 66: *The Annunciation*, detail (14th century). Ely Stained Glass Museum, Ely Cathedral, Cambridgeshire, United Kingdom; Bridgeman Art Library, London and New York.

p. 69: *Psalm 150, Oh Praise God in His Holiness* (1979), Marc Chagall (1887–1985). Chichester Cathedral, Sussex, United Kingdom; Bridgeman Art Library, London and New York. © 2000 Artists Rights Society (ARS), New York/ADAGP, Paris.

p. 70: *December*, from the series *Labors of the Months* (15th century). Victoria and Albert Museum, London, United Kingdom; Art Resource, New York.

p. 73: *Temptation in the Desert*, detail (c. 1225). Originally from the Troyes Cathedral, Paris, France; Victoria and Albert Museum, London, United Kingdom; Bridgeman Art Library, London and New York.

p. 74: *Noah in his Ark*, detail of the dove returning with olive twig (1270–80). Originally from the Church of Wimpffen im Tale. Hessisches Landesmuseum, Darmstadt, Germany. Erich Lessing/Art Resource, New York.

p. 77: *Scenes from the Legend of Saint Nicholas and the Temptation of Christ*, detail (c. 1200). Cathedral of Saint Peter and Saint Paul, Troyes, France; Peter Willi/Bridgeman Art Library, London and New York.

p. 78: *Margarete, Governess of the Netherlands*, detail (16th century). Église de Brou, Bourg-en-Bresse, France; Erich Lessing/Art Resource, New York.

p. 81: *Two Kneeling Angels* (1838). Potosi, Bolivia; Bridgeman Art Library, London and New York.

p. 83: *Ruth Gleaning* (1862), by R. T. Bayne. Sculthorpe Church, Norfolk, United Kingdom; Bridgeman Art Library, London and New York.

p. 84: *Untitled* (1952), by Fernand Leger (1881–1955). Audincourt Church, Besancon, France; Bridgeman Art Library, London and New York. © 2000 Artists Rights Society (ARS), New York/ADAGP, Paris.

p. 87: *Window from the Villa Wulffraat*, by Jacoba van Heemskerck (1876–1923). Haags Gemeentemuseum, Netherlands; Bridgeman Art Library, London and New York.

p. 88: *Saint Cecilia with Palm and Bell* (15th century), British. Church of All Saints, Langport, Somerset, United Kingdom; Bridgeman Art Library, London and New York.

LOVE

p. 90: *Honeymoon of King René of Anjou* (1862), by Sir Edward Burne-Jones (1833–98) and Dante Gabriel Rossetti (1828–82). Victoria and Albert Museum, London, United Kingdom; Bridgeman Art Library, London and New York.

p. 92: *Christ in Majesty*; south rose window, detail (c. 1226). Chartres Cathedral, France; Bridgeman Art Library, London and New York.

p. 95: *Prodigal Son, Curlew River and the Burning Fiery Furnace*, detail (1979), by John Piper (1903–92). Aldeburgh Church, Suffolk, United Kingdom; Bridgeman Art Library, London and New York.

p. 97: *Spring* (1894), by Eugene Samuel Grasset (1841–1917). Musée des Arts Décoratifs, Paris, France; Giraudon/Art Resource, New York.

p. 98: *The Nativity* (1982), by John Piper (1903–92). Iffley Church, Oxfordshire, United Kingdom; Bridgeman Art Library, London and New York.

p. 101: *The Virgin and Child*, detail (c. 1170). Church of Saint Mary and All Saints, Rivenhall, Essex, United Kingdom; Bridgeman Art Library, London and New York.

p. 102: *Saul and David* (1959), by Otto Dix. Private Collection; Bridgeman Art Library, London and New York. © 2000 Artists Rights Society (ARS), New York/ADAGP, Paris.

p. 105: *Madonna and Child* (c. 1380). Sammlung des Reidesfreiherrn Von Stein, Kappenburg, Germany; Bridgeman Art Library, London and New York.

p. 106: *Untitled* (1974), by Marc Chagall (1887–1985). All Saints Church, Tudeley, Kent, United Kingdom; Bridgeman Art Library, London and New York. © 2000 Artists Rights Society (ARS), New York/ADAGP, Paris.

p. 109: *Journey of the Prodigal Son* (1859), by Didron of Paris. Church of Saint Mary, Feltwell, Norfolk, United Kingdom; Bridgeman Art Library, London and New York.

p. 110: *Saint Damian Healing a Lame*, detail (second-half of 13th century), by Master of Saint Francis. Upper Church, San Francesco, Assisi, Italy; Alinari/Art Resource, New York.

p. 113: *Untitled* (c. 1960–70s), by Marc Chagall (1887–1985). All Saints Church, Tudeley, Kent, United Kingdom; Bridgeman Art Library, London and New York. © 2000 Artists Rights Society (ARS), New York/ADAGP, Paris.

p. 114: *Moses and the Golden Calf* (16th century), British. Victoria and Albert Museum, London, United Kingdom; Bridgeman Art Library, London and New York.

p. 117: *Sower* window (12th–13th century). Canterbury Cathedral, Kent, United Kingdom; Bridgeman Art Library, London and New York.

p. 118: *The Prophet Daniel* (15th century). Victoria and Albert Museum, London, United Kingdom; Bridgeman Art Library, London and New York.

p. 121: *Christ Teaching* (13th–14th century). Victoria and Albert Museum, London, United Kingdom; Bridgeman Art Library, London and New York.

p. 123: *The Nativity* (19th century), by Sir Edward Burne-Jones (1833–98). Huish Episcopi, Somerset, United Kingdom; Bridgeman Art Library, London and New York.

p. 124: *The Creation of the Sun and Moon* (15th century). Saint Florentin, near Auxerre, France; Bridgeman Art Library, London and New York.

p. 126: *The Nativity* (1491), after a design attributed to Domenico Ghirlandaio (1449–94). Santa Maria delle Carceri, Prato, Italy; Bridgeman Art Library, London and New York.